Original title:
Vases and Verses

Copyright © 2025 Creative Arts Management OÜ
All rights reserved.

Author: Milo Harrington
ISBN HARDBACK: 978-1-80581-797-0
ISBN PAPERBACK: 978-1-80581-324-8
ISBN EBOOK: 978-1-80581-797-0

Ceramic Whispers of Yesterday

In a shop where time stands still,
Clay heroes dance on windowsills.
A teapot laughs, it spills its tea,
While cups in giggles hide with glee.

One plate recalls a frisky cat,
Who crashed the party, oh! Imagine that.
Like lovers caught in porcelain play,
They break for laughs and roll away.

Artistry Entwined with Nature

A bowl of greens holds guacamole,
But didn't expect a dancing dolly.
With chips on the side, they sway and twist,
In this banquet, no urge to resist.

The pitcher's singing sweet lemonade,
While spoons in harmony serenade.
Nature's bottle with a pop and a fizzle,
Turns afternoon into a fizzy drizzle.

Floral Whispers

A vase wears a crown of daisies bright,
It boasts of springtime, oh what a sight!
But bees in bow ties buzz around,
Stealing smiles without a sound.

Each petal tells a tale or two,
Of mischief and mayhem, just for you.
Though blooms are sweet, they tease and taunt,
As they hold secrets, they won't flaunt.

Echoes in Porcelain

An echo bounces in a china cup,
As spoons stumble, it's time to sup.
Friendly plates, they clink and cheer,
Together they spread laughter here.

The coffee mug hums a tune so bright,
While sugar cubes dance in delight.
In that moment, they kiss the air,
With whims of joy and ceramic flair.

The Artist's Offering

With colors bright, they come alive,
A clumsy sight, they seem to strive.
A painter's brush, a potter's spin,
Creating laughter from within.

A jug so fat, it trips and falls,
A mug that thinks it has big balls.
Each ceramic joke, a playful tease,
Brings joy and giggles with such ease.

Whispers in Glass

In crystal forms, the secrets hide,
A goblet grins, so full of pride.
It tells a joke in bubbles soft,
Floating high and swirling aloft.

The pitcher winks, it knows the score,
While tumblers chat of days of yore.
With every clink, they share a laugh,
In whispers low, amidst the half.

Cultivated Lines

In gardens where the laughter grows,
The pots exchange their witty woes.
A planter boasts of roots so deep,
While silly seeds in soil do leap.

A terracotta laughs, it cracks a grin,
Confessing tales of garden kin.
With every bloom, a quip so fine,
Blooms and giggles intertwine.

Celestial Containers

A cosmic bowl, it spins with glee,
While stars come out for tea, you see.
The mugs hold planets, frothy delights,
Sipping worlds on dreamy nights.

A celestial jar, it bubbles bright,
A comet gleams, quite the sight!
With every sip, a twinkle's shared,
In laughter's flow, we're so ensnared.

Gilded Narratives

In the corner stood a jug,
With a tilt and a playful shrug.
Filled with whispers of old tales,
And a few forgotten snails.

It grinned with its golden sheen,
A sight that was quite obscene.
Sipping stories from its rim,
Where the daylight seemed to swim.

A cat, curious and spry,
Decided it would give it a try.
With a pounce and a leap so bold,
The jug spilled secrets untold.

Later that day, what a mess!
The cat just laughed, oh yes!
For what's life without a spill?
More stories to tell, what a thrill!

Fragrant Fables

A pot of herbs sat on the sill,
Catching scents that gave a thrill.
With basil laughing, mint in chat,
All the while a sneaky rat.

It dreamed of tales from every leaf,
Each moment wrapped in comic grief.
Fennel teased with a zesty wink,
While parsley pondered, deep in pink.

The stories flowed like fragrant tea,
With every sip, pure glee, oh me!
The rat sighed, what a choice to make,
For every word, a tasty flake.

In the end, they cooked a stew,
With laughter that just grew and grew.
Oh, the flavor of friendship's tune,
Brought by herbs beneath the moon!

Blooms of Reflection

In a garden, pots were placed,
Each bloom with a comical face.
A daisy danced with a tiny frown,
While a tulip wore a silly crown.

They chatted 'bout the weather's whim,
Declaring that sunlight's never dim.
But when the rains began to play,
They hid their smiles and fled away.

A squirrel flew by with a nut,
Knocking over the flower cut.
With petals flying everywhere,
They giggled in the fragrant air.

At dusk, with a finale bright,
They sparkled in the fading light.
For flowers know how to have fun,
Turning day's end into a pun!

Glimmering Artifacts

On a shelf, old trinkets gleam,
Each one holds a silly dream.
With a mug holding secrets old,
A laughable tale yet untold.

A spoon once danced in a grand parade,
Until it slipped and made a trade.
It swapped its groove for a lumpy fork,
Now it's stuck in the pot of cork.

Knickknacks whisper through the night,
Sharing glimmers, oh what a sight!
With tales of mischief and of fun,
Echoes of laughter, one by one.

Each artifact a chuckling friend,
With stories that shall never end.
In their shine, the humor flows,
In every crevice, hilarity grows!

The Heart's Repository

In a corner sits a jar,
Filled with dreams and cookies afar.
A little note says 'Take one please,'
But only if you share with bees!

With every crack, a tale is spun,
Of clumsy cats who think it's fun.
They knock it off, it hits the floor,
Now it holds a whole lot more!

A missing lid, a silly grin,
It now collects the dust and din.
Each knick represents a laugh,
A happy dance, a wiggly calf.

So here's a toast to things that break,
And joyous messes we all make.
For in the heart of playful cheer,
A funny tale will always steer.

Lyrical Landscapes

In pots of clay, our thoughts collide,
Each with a frown, but eyes so wide.
Sunflowers sway, with giggles bright,
As they plant puns in morning light.

Oh, paper trails from fallen leaves,
Whisper secrets that no one believes.
A water jug hums a silly tune,
While frogs wear hats beneath the moon.

Every floret tells a jest,
In gardens where we feel our best.
The bees bring news from far and near,
As ants perform their wiggly cheer.

Here's to laughter from the Earth,
In every bloom, a moment's mirth.
Each tangled root and leaf so spry,
A comedy beneath the sky.

The Essence of Embodiment

A jug of giggles, spills on the floor,
With every laugh, it asks for more.
When you pour out the joy inside,
Beware the puddle where fun can slide.

A bowl that claims to hold delight,
Yet rolls around in sheer delight.
Each wobble has a tale to tell,
Of kitchen mishaps that went so well.

A pitcher grins, its spout is wide,
As soda zips and bids goodbye.
It knows too well how fizzes burst,
With bubbly truths that quench our thirst.

Embrace the spills, the flow, the splash,
In frolicsome moments, life will dash.
So raise your cup, your joyful cheer,
For every drop brings laughter near!

Stories in Stone

Old brick and mortar hold a tale,
Of builders' dreams and giddy trails.
Each crack a giggle, each chip a song,
In this funny fortress, we all belong.

A stone statue strikes a pose,
Winking at folks, of whom it knows.
With arms folded in a playful way,
It smiles at watchers, come what may.

Pebbles roll away with grace,
A game of tag, a stone's embrace.
Each gravel laugh, a charming spree,
As we all gather 'neath the tree.

So here's to rocks that won't be tame,
With stories etched, they seek acclaim.
For life's a garden, wild and bold,
With laughter woven through the cold.

Quiet Reflections

In the corner, a pot sings,
Filled with dreams and silly things.
A cactus dons a tiny hat,
Who knew plants could be so sprat?

Sipping tea with blooms so bright,
Whispers of green in the morning light.
Curious ferns chat in glee,
Making jokes for you and me.

Mismatched petals dance in pairs,
Telling tales of their past affairs.
A bulbous one, trying to rhyme,
Trip on the words, oh what a crime!

Reflections sound like laughter loud,
In this garden, I'm quite proud.
Every clay lip grins with flair,
Life is fun in this flowered square.

Shapes of Serenity

A jug round and stout hears the cheer,
Its funky shape draws all near.
On the shelf, an urn with style,
Winks at a bowl that tries to smile.

In the sunlight, shadows collide,
As teapots and pitchers take a ride.
Laughing together, what a sight,
Mixing colors, pure delight!

A vase once tried to wear a bow,
But fell over—oh, what a show!
Lids and knobs play peek-a-boo,
Chasing dust with a mind so true.

Shapes abound in joyful dance,
Every corner shares a chance.
In this play of form and cheer,
All find love in edges clear.

Verdant Verses

Emerald leaves in a rhyming mood,
Whisper tales of their leafy brood.
Pots gossip lightly, trunks sway slow,
Through the laughter, old roots grow.

A fuchsia bloom with a penchant for rhyme,
Flirts with a thistle, oh! What a crime!
In the background, the soil hums,
To tune of the pitter-pat of tiny drums.

Laughter bubbles in the sunlight's grace,
A dandelion wearing a lacy lace.
Spreading seeds with a jolly air,
Making wishes float, everywhere!

With every twist and every bend,
Nature's jesters, they never end.
A garden's giggle, sweet as can be,
Lines of green in humorous spree.

Fragments of Florals

Petals twirl in a comedic spree,
Bouncing round like they're wild and free.
A sunflower's laugh fills the air,
While a daisy plots a prank—beware!

A small posy claims to be tough,
Flexing stems, but don't call its bluff!
When a breeze stirs up a playful fight,
All the buds join in, day or night.

The hydrangeas all wear hats so fine,
Joking about their bold design.
One melts down like a drip of dew,
Leaving a joke sticky but true.

In fragments found among the clatter,
Blooms giggle soft with a joyful chatter.
Roses chuckle, then sigh with cheer,
In the funny game of flora here.

The Poetry of Stillness

In the corner sits a jar,
Who knows just how bizarre.
It claims to hold a secret art,
Yet nothing springs from its heart.

Dust collects upon its face,
A joke of time and empty space.
It winks when you walk by,
As if to say, "I'm quite the sly!"

Chasing thoughts like buzzing bees,
This stillness laughs, it aims to tease.
With every glance, it holds a grin,
Who knew such silence could begin?

So here's to pots both tall and wide,
With chuckles trapped deep inside.
In stillness, laughter takes a stand,
A quiet feast, a funny brand!

Blossoming Bottles of Thought

Bottles line the kitchen shelf,
Each one claiming to be itself.
One claims to hold profound dreams,
But all it does is gather beams.

A bottle swears it knows the cure,
For hair that's wild, and thoughts unsure.
Yet with every twist and pop,
It spills the tea and makes a plop!

Sunflowers dance within the glass,
Trying hard to take some sass.
"I'm here to brighten up your day,
If only I could find my way!"

So let them laugh and spill their brew,
With secrets vibrant, bright, and true.
In bottles, thoughts may twist and sway,
While humor blooms in bright array!

Whimsical Recollections of Form

A teapot dreams of waltzing tea,
While serving cups all sit with glee.
Yet misshaped spouts, they dance askew,
No one quite knows what to do.

Chubby mugs with silly grins,
Play charades of distant sins.
"Do I hold coffee or a laugh?
Why not both?" declares the chaff!

The pitcher fumbles, spills a song,
Remembers when it once belonged.
To days of laughter, joy on tap,
Echoes now in every gap.

To gather shapes of light and fun,
Embracing laughter, everyone!
In playful antics, forms unite,
Whimsical tales of pure delight!

Curated Still Lifes of Emotion

An apple sighs upon the plate,
While grapes chuckle at their fate.
"Are we still life, or just a joke?
Let's mix it up, and have a smoke!"

Bananas know they're here to flaunt,
With curves so fine, they love to taunt.
"Who's for a split?" they softly yell,
While laughter spreads just like a spell.

Pineapples wear those crowns so proud,
As if to say, "I'm cool, I'm loud!"
In sunny hues, emotions play,
A fruit parade, oh what a day!

So gather round, both sweet and sour,
In this still-life, we find our power.
With every glance, the humor shines,
Curated feelings, love, and vines!

Silent Echoes

In a room full of flowers, quite neat,
A cat claimed a vase for a seat.
The blooms all swayed in delight,
As the feline relaxed, what a sight!

A dog watched with envy, perplexed,
Wishing he too was less vexed.
With a wag and a hop of his tail,
He tried to squeeze in, but he'd fail!

The flowers giggled with glee,
At the antics they'd see on the spree.
A bird perched high, chirped loudly,
"That's just how we roll, quite proudly!"

In this madcap parade of mirth,
Where pets vie for comfort and worth.
Each bloom in the vase felt so grand,
While chaos danced, hand in hand.

Blossoms in Abundance

A bee flew in, buzzing with zeal,
Landed on a daisy, oh what a deal!
He tried to impress with his hums so fine,
But stumbled on petals, oh how they whined!

Meanwhile, a squirrel scurried about,
In a hat made of leaves, shouting out.
"I'm the king of the park," he declared,
As the daisies below all stared, unprepared.

A turtle in shades thought it was fab,
To watch the chaos, while holding a crab.
"Life's a show on this grassy patch,"
He wrote a review, and signed with a scratch.

With laughter like sunshine, the garden thrived,
Where silliness blossomed and all felt alive.
A rabbit in ribbons hopped through the scene,
And all went wild, getting loud and keen.

Veiled Verses

In a cupboard hidden from sight,
Lived a sock puppet with dreams of flight.
He wrote poems in secret, so grand,
While the towels all rolled their eyes on demand.

A teapot chimed in, full of sass,
"Don't be absurd, you're made of glass!"
Yet every time tea was brewed with grace,
The puppet's verses would take up space.

With a whisk's bright whisking, they whispered away,
Crafting stories of cups that never decay.
A colander sighed, "Just let it out,"
As the drawers sighed on, with laughter and doubt.

In this humorous rally of kitchen dreams,
Where clattering spoons were the loudest screams,
Each line crafted stumbled, yet shone,
In this world where the mundane feels like home.

Essence of Eternity

In a time-worn hall with jesters and japes,
Grapes told tales to curious shapes.
A pear wearing spectacles squinted to see,
And chuckled aloud, 'What a sight, oh me!'

A clock chimed in, tick-tock it paced,
While lemons danced sweetly, all lemony-faced.
The oranges giggled at every slip,
As nuts rolled around, each one on a trip.

Out through the window, a honeybee leaped,
Spreading laughter, as blossoms all wept.
"Join in the fun," they all loudly yelled,
And thus through the halls, silliness swelled.

Each fruit and clock sang with glee,
About moments of joy that were meant to be.
In this blend of laughter, a feast of delight,
Where time flies by in the silliest flight.

Whispers of Porcelain Dreams

In a world where teacups chat,
They spill their gossip as they sat.
A sugar bowl with quite a grin,
Says, 'Watch out, the spoons might spin!'

A saucer giggles, oh so sweet,
While telling tales of last night's feat.
A broken mug just shakes her head,
And calls them all a bunch of bread!

The kettle whistles, joining in,
With jokes about a ceramic twin.
They clink and clatter, full of cheer,
As porcelain dreams draw ever near.

But should a chip appear, they cry,
'Oh, what a blow, I fear to die!'
Yet all just laugh, for who can frown,
When cups unite in porcelain town?

Echoes in Glazed Silence

The plates are dancing, what a sight,
With forks and knives, they laugh with spite.
A soup bowl winks, its contents bold,
'If I were you, I'd never mold!'

A butter dish, so slick and sly,
Claims it knows the reason why.
The ladle leaps in playful glee,
Singing songs of soups and tea.

While coffee mugs just roll their eyes,
And whisper 'Is that all your prize?'
For in this silence, echoes ring,
Of tales of food and endless spring.

But should a spoon drop to the floor,
They shout, 'Now that's an uproar!'
In glazed silence, laughter swells,
As stories spin like magic spells.

Cradled Beauty in Clay

Oh, the pots declare a joyous day,
With flowers bright in every sway.
A terracotta laughs so loud,
'Look at me, I'm very proud!'

A pitcher spins, a whirlwind grand,
Says, 'Pour some fun, and take a stand!'
With every drip, the petals sway,
Making each moment a holiday.

The planters jest with roots entwined,
In their embrace, the fun aligned.
'Trust the soil, let secrets grow,
With every bud, let laughter flow!'

And when the glaze begins to shine,
They gather 'round, their jokes divine.
For beauty cradled in a sway,
Delights in laughter every day.

Petals and Poetry entwined

In a garden filled with laughs and puns,
Where flowers chat and chase the suns.
A daisy whispers, 'Join the fun,'
'Our verses blend until we run!'

The tulips sway in poetic grace,
Each petal dances, finds its place.
They spin in rhyme, creating cheer,
With every bloom, a joke appears.

The roses chuckle, full of sass,
While daisies roll around the grass.
Fluttering leaves complete the scene,
As laughter blooms, both bright and green.

And when the moonlight graces all,
They gather 'round, they start to call.
With petals soft, and poetry bright,
They share their dreams throughout the night.

Poetry in Petal Form

In gardens where giggles bloom,
A flower's hat took up some room.
The bees wore ties, oh what a sight,
Polka-dotted pants, so full of light.

The daisies danced without a care,
Their laughter drifted through the air.
Lilies threw a party at night,
With buzzing tunes that felt so right.

Roses joked of love's fine art,
While thorns played darts, oh what a start.
The sun joined in with a bright grin,
As petals laughed 'neath the chagrin.

So come, dear friend, let's join the fun,
In nature's jest, we're never done.
With petals bright and hearts so warm,
We'll weave our words in playful form.

The Dreamer's Vessel

Once in a dream a pitcher spoke,
With a sense of humor that softly woke.
It told of swims in puddles bright,
And sails on clouds, what a silly flight!

A teacup laughed at a stony mug,
Claiming it needed a cheerful hug.
They made a bet on who could shine,
With lemon drops and peppermint wine.

The spoon chimed in, "Let's have a race,
In this kitchen, we'll find our place."
Forks took bets, with glee in their eyes,
Over who'd win, oh what a surprise!

As sugar sprinkled on top with grace,
Each corner of laughter had its space.
In this funny dream of cups and cheer,
The dreamer found solace, sweet and clear.

Sturdy Hold of Solace

A sturdy cup with chipped gray rim,
Claimed he was tough, though slightly dim.
"I hold the tea that warms your soul,
While others spill, I pay the toll."

The saucer countered, "I'm classier, see,
Without my charm, you'd just be tea!"
They bickered along their wooden stage,
A comical sight, quite all the rage.

A wobbly chair joined the heated bout,
Hoping for laughs, but filled with doubt.
"Without me, you'd spill, oh what a shame,
So let's all laugh and play the game."

Together they found a lighter way,
To make big fusses of mundane play.
For in their flaws, the truth was told,
A sturdy hold of laughter, pure gold.

Glass and Grace

In a cabinet high, where cobwebs climb,
Stood a glass jar, a treasure of time.
It whispered jokes with a rattle and clink,
"This wild life made me start to think!"

With marbles inside, it spun tales so grand,
Of a dancing frog in a faraway land.
Each bounce it took brought giggles galore,
As the jar held secrets, oh what a score!

A paperweight said, "You're way too bright,
But I'm the one that keeps things tight."
Together they laughed at how odd they seemed,
In a world where glasses effortlessly dreamed.

So here's to the glass, so full of grace,
For in its curves, we find our place.
Through silly whispers and clinking cheer,
In this playful art, we draw you near.

The Dance of Art and Anemones

In a studio of colors bright,
A paint splatter took to flight.
Anemones wiggled in grand delight,
As laughter twirled, oh what a sight!

Brushes dipped in hues asinine,
They danced like clowns on a tangled line.
Each stroke a giggle, each mix divine,
Creating a masterpiece that's borderline!

Palette whirled in joyful spree,
While petals chuckled with glee.
Who knew that art could be so free?
It's just a party, come paint with me!

So grab a canister and tag along,
In this crazy dance, you can't go wrong.
Join the shindig, we'll sing a song,
With anemones and art, we all belong!

Silenced Stories of the Fired Heart

In a kiln where secrets hide,
Clay pots whisper, filled with pride.
They dream of bubbles, and fates deride,
In a world of heat, with love applied.

Once they're molded, so tenderly,
Waiting for flames to set them free.
Pottery vows, 'Just wait and see!'
But with each roar, they bounce with glee.

Cracks appear, they give a laugh,
Each one a tale of their own path.
They can't be silenced, just do the math,
Firing up stories with a witty quaff!

So raise a mug, let's toast tonight,
To the pots that giggle from their plight.
In the chaos of heat, they take to flight,
Fired hearts dancing in pure delight!

Clarity in the Midst of Chaos

In a room where socks seek socks,
Amidst the pile, reality knocks.
Chaos reigns, but in it, I box
A laugh, a giggle, that clearly rocks!

Messy desks tell tales untold,
Sticky notes in colors bold.
Yet amidst the clutter, visions unfold,
As clarity dances, all drip-dry old.

Coffee cups and scattered pens,
Life is tangled, just now and then.
Finding laughter, time's true friend,
In this jumble, get lost again!

So embrace the chaos, jump on in,
Where clarity's a laugh, and life's a win.
A joyful mess—let's spin and spin,
In the chaos, where fun begins!

Heartbeats in Brimming Brevity

Tiny hearts in jars of glass,
They beat a tune, oh what a blast!
In moments short, their joys amass,
A flickering dance, oh how they flash!

Each pulse a giggle, a fleeting jest,
Brevity shines, it feels the best.
Time ticks on with playful zest,
In the tiny beats, we find our quest.

Laughter echoed in each small thump,
Short-lived bliss, but oh, what a jump!
Like fireflies in the night, they clump,
Creating joy with every pump!

So treasure small moments, hold them tight,
For in brevity, there's pure delight.
With tiny heartbeats, take your flight,
Catch the laughter, 'til day turns to night!

Blooming Upon Stillness

A pot of flowers, plump and bright,
Swaying gently, what a sight!
In every color, wild and free,
Whispering secrets to the bee.

One day a breeze, a feathered tease,
Knocked over stems with all the ease.
They danced like corks upon the floor,
And laughed, as petals begged for more.

They tumbled down with quite a cheer,
"Oh look at us, we've lost our fear!"
Giggling down in disarray,
We bloomed anew in a funny way.

So here's to blooms that dare to flop,
In moments brief, let laughter stop.
For even when they lose their ground,
Life in chaos is joy profound.

Serenade of the Shattered

A clumsy hand with much to boast,
Picked up the cup he loved the most.
It slipped away, oh what a fright,
A symphony of shatters bright.

Each piece a note, a cheeky sound,
As fragments scattered all around.
The cat sat back, with wide-eyed glee,
"Is this a concert just for me?"

In every sliver, a tale unfolds,
A jazzy jig, as laughter rolls.
The spoon joined in with a clang and bang,
As pots and pans began to sang.

Oh how we chuckle at the mess,
The joy of chaos, we confess!
For every crack and crumb in sight,
Is music made from sheer delight.

Hold My Words Beneath Glass

A jar of thoughts, so bright and bold,
In glass confines, their tales retold.
"Let's seal these dreams," they chant in glee,
But who is to know when they flee?

With tiny notes, they wiggle and sway,
"Open us up, we want to play!"
A wiggly worm with quite the grin,
Invites them out for a merry spin.

With every twist, a giggle's freed,
As words come out to plant a seed.
A dance begins, in fits and starts,
With laughter shared, they steal our hearts.

So hold them tight, these dreams of ours,
In laughter's light, like glowing stars.
For under glass, they yearn to leap,
From silly thoughts, the joy we keep.

The Symphony of Shards

In a cupboard high, a treasure trove,
Of porcelain dreams, and whispers rove.
Each plate and cup a story spun,
Until the day when two did run.

A chase ensued, oh what a sight!
As laughter echoed into the night.
One slipped, one fell, oh dear, oh no!
And thus began the shard-filled show.

They twinkled under a light so bright,
Like a disco ball, in sheer delight.
The broom came in, to sweep, to laugh,
Collecting jewels from their mishap.

Yet in the end, we sing their tune,
These broken pieces, like a cartoon.
For every crack tells a tale divine,
In laughter's key, our hearts entwine.

Claybound Lyrics

In a pot painted bright, with a goofball face,
They hold all my dreams in a charming embrace.
With flowers that giggle and dance in delight,
Each petal a punchline, oh what a sight!

Tea towels are fancied, they rest by the kettle,
Whistling and wobbling, they bounce like a metal.
As I pour in the laughs, the cup laughs right back,
A clumsy ballet, never losing its track!

Tranquil Artistry

A jug on the shelf, wearing a hat full of quirks,
It hums silly tunes while adjusting its jerks.
With wisdom of clay and a smirk all its own,
It tells me sweet stories, quite cheeky and grown!

The brushes all gossip, in colors so bright,
Sliding and gliding, creating pure light.
With acrylics and oils, they have quite the brawl,
In a canvas duel over who paints the wall!

Repose in Rhyme

A bowl with a giggle holds snacks just for fun,
While spoons start to dance, like they're out on the run.
They bob and they weave with a swagger so spry,
As popcorn bursts forth, oh my, oh my!

With crumbs all around, the table's a mess,
Yet laughter rings true, no need to confess.
Sippy cups chatter, jocular and round,
In this whimsical world, pure joy is profound!

The Poet's Chalice

A goblet that trembles on legs made of rhyme,
It quips about poets who dance out of time.
Each sip is a joke, oh what splendid surprise,
With laughter like bubbles, it tickles the eyes!

The coaster is grinning while holding it steady,
With coasters like these, each toast is quite ready.
Raise high all your mugs, let joy overflow,
In this happy toast, let the quirks brightly show!

Sentiments in Shadow

In a corner sits my pot,
A relic of a crafty plot.
Filled with crumbs and bits of fluff,
It proudly claims its silly stuff.

Oh, what joy in mismatched pairs,
A cactus here, a sock that dares!
Dreams of flowers, bright and bold,
Yet all it holds is tales retold.

My friends all laugh, they point and tease,
"Is that your home for wayward peas?"
I sigh and nod, a smile I wear,
For in this mess, I find my flair.

So here's to pots that hold the strange,
Filled with whims that love to change.
In every laugh, in every joke,
Lies beauty in the chaos woke.

The Keeper of Thoughts

Within my room, a jar does gleam,
It captures every wish and dream.
Yet all it keeps are points and puns,
A treasure trove of silly runs.

I toss in socks and crumpled notes,
Conversations that raise hot votes.
When found again, what do I see?
A cabbage thought, or was it me?

It guards my laughter, holds my frowns,
Dances around in silly gowns.
A keeper of this jumbled fun,
I'll feed it more, it's just begun!

So let it grow, my quirky stash,
With giggles caught in every flash.
A jar of nonsense, a joy to bring,
In this odd world, I am the king!

Elegance of Embellishments

On a shelf, a potted grin,
Covered with soil and a woollen skin.
It winks at me when I pass by,
With a leaf that looks like it can fly!

A sprinkle of paint, a dash of cheer,
Adorning odd shapes that appear near.
A snail once tried to climb so high,
Only to slip and wave goodbye!

Oh, the goldfish bowl holds genuine laughs,
Accidental art from bubbly drafts.
With glitter and glue, the madness swirls,
Where every blunder effectively twirls.

So let's toast to the odd and bright,
In this parade of fun-filled sight.
For elegance shines when mishaps bloom,
In our joyful, quirky room!

Scribed Serenity

A mug of thoughts, half full, half spilled,
Jots down dreams the mind has thrilled.
Pasted ribbons and cheerful stains,
Caught within, the joy remains.

Each scribed line, a memory laced,
In whimsical words of warmth embraced.
Yet among the wisdom, surprises grow,
Like the cat's paw who steals the show!

I write of clouds and wiggly worms,
Pages filled with fanciful turns.
Lost in scribbles, I sway and sigh,
Is that a poem or a pizza pie?

So here's to stories that never cease,
To the playful spirit that brings us peace.
In every blunder, a tale unfurled,
With the laughter, we shape our world!

The Symphony of Stillness

In a room filled with flair, not a sound to be found,
Sit the objects of beauty, where silence is crowned.
A vase plays a tune, with its floral bouquet,
It sways to the rhythm of each passing day.

But a giggle escapes from a pot on the shelf,
"I'm not just a planter, I'm a poet myself!"
With a wink and a nod, it starts telling jokes,
About blooming mishaps and watering blokes.

A water jar chuckles at the vase's grand plight,
"Who needs a refill? Just wheel me tonight!"
Flora dancing around, with the sun shining bright,
All join the party, an absurd, silly sight.

So here's to the stillness, where laughter does bloom,
In a world that is quiet, there's joy to consume.
Let's toast with a teacup, and bright spirits soar,
For in this odd silence, we're never a bore.

Petal-Wrapped Dreams

A petal unwrapped from a curious bud,
Whispers of giggles while stuck in the mud.
"I dreamed I was dancing in a grand ball tonight,
But look at me now, what a pitiful sight!"

The daisies all snicker, as bees buzz along,
Humming a tune of a flower's old song.
"Why wear fancy dresses? A tutu is fine!
Just strut with your petals, and really, you'll shine!"

A rose in a top hat brings humor to light,
"Come join the parade! To a petal-filled night!"
With stems in the air and pollen galore,
They dance through the garden, a floral uproar!

So garlands and laughter twirl into the breeze,
As petals embark on their whimsical tease.
Let dreams be unwrapped in this absurd little scene,
Where flowers unite in each silly routine.

Jar of Journeying

A jar on a shelf, filled to the brim,
With traveled tales, not too stout, not too slim.
"Oh, where have I been? The stories, they flow!
From deserts to mountains, I'm quite the know-show!"

An old coffee mug pipes in with a grin,
"Let me tell you, my friend, about where I've been!
I once held hot brews, but I dreamt of the sea,
Now I float on the waves, can I go home with thee?"

The jar rolls its eyes, but it can't help but laugh,
"Every journey's a trip, just like a warm bath!
So come gather around, let's swap what we can,
From marshmallow clouds to a wild rainbow plan!"

So gather the close ones, in this jar we confide,
With journeys and journeys, we abide side by side.
From porcelain tales to adventures absurd,
The stories keep flowing; let's share every word!

Rhythms in the Garden

In a patch of bright colors where giggles prevail,
A garden of chaos begins its own tale.
With gnomes doing cartwheels and flowers that sway,
This garden of nonsense is here for the play!

The daisies all shout, with their petals ablaze,
"Let's have a dance party in this floral maze!"
The sunflowers nod, with their tall, waving heads,
"Let's rhythm our way through the dreams in our beds!"

A watering can trills, with a jingle so sweet,
"Tap-tap on the ground, let's keep up the beat!"
While a butterfly swoops, dressed in glittering hues,
"I'll lead this parade, can I wear all your shoes?"

As the moon rises high, laughter echoes the skies,
With rhymes and with rhythms that dance in disguise.
In this garden of joy, where the silly runs free,
Life's bright little moments give magic to glee!

The Beauty of Stillness

In corners they sit, all dressed in clay,
Gathering dust like it's a play.
One shout of laughter, they start to shake,
Echoes of giggles make them quake.

They're empty yet full, a curious bunch,
Holding strange secrets, always a hunch.
If they could speak, what tales they'd weave,
Of flowers they cradled, then had to leave.

With a wobbly smile, they stand so proud,
Who needs a crowd when you're this loud?
An artistic mess, a quirky delight,
Their silence breaks, laughter takes flight.

In the stillness, the fun unfolds,
Cracks and chips, their stories retold.
Like comedians caught in a frown,
Their charm is the best in this quirky town.

Echoing Blooms

Petals and echoes, what a fine pair,
Floating on whispers without a care.
The blooms start to giggle, a chuckle or two,
Joining a dance in the morning dew.

A garden of smiles, oh what a sight,
Filling the air with pure delight.
Each color a joke that brightens the day,
As they trade silly quips in their own way.

The bees join in, they're buzzing in tune,
Hoping to catch a flower's cartoon.
This comedy of nature, so sweet and silly,
Makes even the grumpiest gardener want to be silly.

Under the sun, they weave their tale,
With whispers of laughter that never pale.
A bouquet of joy in every sway,
Echoing blooms in a droll ballet.

Poetic Potpourri

A splash of colors in a humble bowl,
Each petal and leaf, a comedic goal.
Whiff of mischief in the fragrant air,
Tales of enchantment, scents of flair.

Every whiff a giggle, every mix a pun,
Crafted by nature, all in good fun.
Laughter wafts high, like a whispering breeze,
Telling the world to chuckle with ease.

In a blend of aromas, stories arise,
Tickling the nose with sweet surprise.
With each dash and sprinkle, humor does bloom,
In this potpourri of silly perfume.

So let's have a party, come join the cheer,
In this fragrant delight, there's nothing to fear.
For in every essence, you'll find a good jest,
A poetic concoction that's simply the best.

Shapes of Silence

In quiet stillness, they stand and grin,
Holding their breath for a cheeky spin.
Shapes of silence hold stories galore,
While laughter tickles just outside the door.

Curves and angles, a playful tease,
Winking at shadows that dance with ease.
Each form a character, unique and grand,
Waiting for mischief to take a stand.

Their quietness crackles, like a lively spark,
Amidst the giggles, in daylight's park.
Shaped like a joke, but still so calm,
In this world of humor, they hold the charm.

When the night creeps in, and laughter decays,
They make funny faces, in unexpected ways.
In all their stillness, the wildness lies,
The shapes of silence, where the funny stuff flies.

The Garden's Alabaster Song

In the garden where flowers bloom,
A pot's too big, it takes up room.
Yet with a grin and a clever way,
It holds the weeds, come what may.

A jug with charm, it's quite a catch,
Though on its side, the flowers stretch.
It smiles at raindrops, giggles in the sun,
A clumsy dance, oh, what fun!

Leaves are chatting, roots are prancing,
Even the stones seem to be glancing.
The fountain laughs, the daisies tease,
All join the pot, with flair and ease.

So let them sing their silly tune,
With every bloom, the garden's boon.
Each vessel's joke makes spirits lift,
A happy pot is nature's gift!

Curves of Contained Thoughts

Round and plump, a pot so wise,
Hiding secrets, what a surprise!
A twist of fate, a twist of clay,
The thoughts inside just sway and play.

An awkward jar, with a silly base,
Stands proud and tall, in a funny space.
It wobbles here and dances there,
With dreams of muffins—so debonair!

Doodles drawn, on polished sides,
A lopsided smile that giggly hides.
It whispers tales of lemonade,
Mistakes of love, and promises made.

Oh, these curves, they laugh and share,
With every drip, a fragrant air.
In every nook, a chuckle found,
In witty clay, our bonds abound!

Reflections in Earthen Elegance

A bowl of earth, with stories vast,
Holds crumbs of past and memories cast.
It reflects a life of highs and lows,
With every chip, more laughter grows.

Bright flowers blush, peeking inside,
With looks of wonder, they can't hide.
The vessel twirls, a dance of cheer,
In humor's grip, it holds them near.

Mismatched curls, a handle askew,
Bears the weight of moments new.
With gentle cracks that make it dear,
Each flaw tells tales of joy and fear.

Oh, ceramic dreams, let's raise a toast,
To all the pots that we love most.
In gaiety clad, they spin and sway,
In every glimpse, we find our play!

Crafted Secrets of the Heart

In a corner, a quirky cup,
Sips of laughter, never giving up.
It spills out jokes, with a clatter and clang,
Filling the room with a merry twang.

A teapot stout, bears a silly grin,
With tales of sugar and a splash of gin.
Pour it out boldly, don't let it fester,
In every drop, there's love to invest-er.

A pitcher jests with curves so fine,
Laughing aloud, it's happy design.
It splashes joy in every face,
Inviting all to join the race.

So here we toast to all that's cute,
To every cup, and every flute.
In crafted pots, our secrets lie,
With laughter's echo, we touch the sky!

Sips of Serenity in a Bowl

In a bowl of quirky shapes,
My soup's having a dance break!
Frothy bubbles wear funny hats,
Sipping laughter with tiny rats.

Ladle wins the game and spins,
Juggling noodles, it grins,
Slurps echo 'round the table,
As broccoli joins, quite unstable.

Chopsticks try a tricky twirl,
Wiggling like a dizzy girl,
Every taste, a giggle, a sight,
When dinner's served, no room for spite!

So let's soup it up, the fun's not shy,
With giggles simmering as we try,
In this bowl of joy, each gulp a cheer,
A feast of laughter, endless and clear.

Expression in the Curved Form

Curvy shapes upon the shelf,
They giggle, too, these pots of self,
One's all round, another's square,
Flirting with fruits, without a care.

At breakfast, toast becomes a star,
Slipping through the butter jar,
"Look at me!" the bread exclaims,
As jams create some silly names.

Stirring spoons with silly swirls,
Whisking dreams like dancing girls,
In the kitchen, laughter brews,
Chunky veggies wearing shoes!

So gather round, embrace the fun,
This kitchen's parties have just begun,
With curves that charm and spoons that sing,
Each dish is art, let joy take wing!

Adorned with Timeless Remains

Old relics on the mantle stand,
Winking with a ghostly hand,
A teapot with a charming pout,
What secrets does it hold about?

Cobwebs dance, a ballet grand,
While dusty books form a band,
Pages flip, they giggle low,
Telling tales of long ago.

An ancient clock, its ticks like jokes,
Poking fun at sleepy folks,
Time laughs loud, escapes its cage,
Each tick a line, a funny page!

In corners, laughter twists and twirls,
With every trinket, glee unfurls,
A timeless charm in the silly scenes,
Where past and present laugh, it seems.

Threads of Light and Form

Sunlight spills like golden seams,
Through the window, it gleams,
Casting shadows, dancing bright,
On fabrics that giggle with delight.

A curtain whispering a joke,
Waving to the sofa, bespoke,
Where cushions puff and smile wide,
Inviting you to take a ride!

Threads of light weave tales that play,
As sunlight pirouettes in a sway,
Every shade a chuckle shared,
In a fabric world, laughter's bared!

So let's stitch the fun with glee,
In every fold, a memory,
Weaving joy from dusk till dawn,
In this tapestry, we all belong!

Versed in Bloom

In the garden, pots take flight,
With flowers dancing left and right.
A tulip snickers, a daisy grins,
While potted plants swap silly sins.

A cactus tells a joke so prickly,
His punchlines always come out quickly.
The roses roll their eyes in fun,
While daisies laugh, their petals spun.

The lilies gossip in the breeze,
Sharing secrets among the trees.
Each bloom a verse, a quirky tale,
In this garden, we must not fail.

So grab a pot, and let it show,
With laughter sprouting, let it grow!
For every bloom that lifts a jest,
Brings joy to life, it's simply best!

The Harmony of Clay

In a studio where pots reside,
Clay and laughter both collide.
A hefty bowl starts cracking jokes,
While tiny cups spread giggly pokes.

A pitcher sings a silly tune,
As spoons and forks all dance by moon.
The clay spins round, a merry dance,
Each piece with charm, a silly chance.

With swirling shapes, the humor flows,
As mugs and plates all share their woes.
The wheel just laughs, it spins so fast,
Creating joy that's bound to last.

In this clay world, just have some fun,
Where pots unite, and joy's begun!
Each crack and curve, a smile does bring,
In harmony, we laugh and sing!

Scripted Silhouettes

In shadows cast by moonlight's grace,
The outlines dance, a funny chase.
A teapot stirs with a cheeky wink,
While wine glasses giggle, don't you think?

The shadows play as if they're friends,
Creating stories that never ends.
A plate whispers, a cup replies,
Together spinning wild, oh my!

The forks play tag with spoons at night,
Making mischief, what a sight!
The laughter echoes in the dark,
With every shape, there's a spark.

These silhouettes of joy and cheer,
Bring out the giggles, far and near.
So let your shadows dance and prance,
In scripted fun, let's take a chance!

A Garden of Expressions

Amidst the blooms, there grows a laugh,
As bees wear hats, the flowers craft.
A sunflower hums a jaunty tune,
While daisies giggle under the moon.

The tulips dressed in color bright,
Crack jokes on bumblebees in flight.
Each petal's wink, a playful tease,
In this garden, all find ease.

The wilting weeds share wild old tales,
Of Earth's great winds and playful gales.
Each stem a story waiting to sprout,
With hearty chuckles as they shout.

A garden filled with smiles galore,
Where blooms and jokes forever soar!
So stop a while, just take a peek,
In nature's jest, it's joy we seek!

The Essence Encased

In a pot of porcelain, a flower dreams,
It whispers secrets in buttery beams.
With petals like laughter, they dance and sway,
While squirrels debate on the average day.

A cat walks by, judging the scene,
With eyes that twinkle, oh so obscene.
'Why the fuss over blooms in a bowl?'
She chuckles softly, her heart taking a toll.

A ladybug joins, with swagger and air,
'What's a petal to a bug without flair?'
She spins and twirls, creating her song,
But the vase wobbles—oh, where did she go wrong?

In this circus of giggles, the room has a flair,
Where laughter is blooming, without any care.
An ensemble of quirks in a sunny old nook,
Here's to the fun, in our wild little book!

Heartfelt Hanamichi

On a stage painted bright, a pot takes a bow,
While roots tickle the soil, saying, 'Look at me now!'
A bumblebee buzzes, sets the scene right,
With a pollen-packed punch, bringing pure delight.

The tulips perform like a rock concert band,
While daisies do flips, isn't nature just grand?
A sunflower's grinning, with its head in the sun,
Declaring each moment's a wild, frothy fun!

The audience giggles, their hearts filled with cheer,
As raindrops start falling—'Oh no, time to clear!'
Yet the laughter persists, as everyone slips,
A comedy sketch of unplanned little trips.

And as dusk begins knocking, the stage dims its light,
Our floral cast yawns, bringing day to a night.
They'll return with the morn, in spectacular grace,
For who could resist such a whimsical place?

Cradled Verse

In a nested corner lives a quirky old mug,
With coffee-stained dreams and a fluffy old rug.
It cradles sweet whispers of stories untold,
And dances on countertops, cheeky and bold.

Next to the spoon, with a flick and a twirl,
A tiny teapot spins, giving tea pots a curl.
'Pour me a potion of giggles and cheer!'
It chirps with delight, 'Oh darlings, I'm here!'

A whisk joins the party, with an electric zap,
Stirring the essence of love like a map.
'Let's shake our troubles, let's shimmy and sway!'
And the cups clink in laughter, brightening the day.

They humor each other, a merry brigade,
In this cozy kitchen, where mishaps cascade.
With splashes of joy, and quips that defy,
They sing their sweet verses as the days flutter by.

Timeless Talismans

Gathered in corners, cutest trinkets of old,
With winks and with smiles, their stories unfold.
A frog in a jar croaks, 'I'm here for the jokes!'
While a gnome in the garden giggles at folks.

The clock ticks in rhythms, all wobbly and weird,
Announcing the moments all treasured and cheered.
'Time is a painter,' hums a rusty key,
'Every chime is a brushstroke on life's tapestry!'

A bottle of marbles, with colors galore,
Shakes with a laughter, 'Let's roll on the floor!'
And stories collide like a raucous parade,
Exploding with whimsy in mischief displayed.

These artifacts hold the giggles of time,
A world of their own, in perfect past rhyme.
So, toast to the treasures that make our hearts dance,
In the realm where the silly and sacred glance.

Bloom and Rhyme

In a garden, pots do dance,
Each petal takes a silly chance.
They twirl and spin, quite a sight,
As bees chuckle, buzzing with delight.

Sunflowers wear their tall top hats,
While daisies gossip like old bats.
The roses blush, oh what a tease,
In this floral party, laughter's a breeze.

Pansies tell jokes, so punchy and bright,
While tulips nod, agreeing outright.
Each color laughs in pure delight,
As morning dew takes its flight.

So come and join this floral spree,
Where giggles sprout like roots from a tree.
In every bloom, a tale unfolds,
In this garden of humor, joy never gets old.

The Language of Blossoms

Petunias whisper secrets so sweet,
With petals like confetti, they skip and greet.
They giggle and chuckle, a riot of cheer,
In this floral mess, not a single tear.

Lilies bow and strike a pose,
While violets play coy, striking a rose.
Each tulip competes with a colorful grin,
As bumblebees buzz, drawn into the din.

The sun claps its hands, lighting the scene,
As marigolds prance, all dressed in green.
The blooms converse in a silly ballet,
Where laughter and color dance in a play.

So listen closely, their chatter is bright,
In the language of blooms, all feels just right.
Join in the fun, let giggles compose,
A symphony of blossoms, where joy overflows.

Still Life in Stanzas

A pitcher grins with a cheeky smile,
Artistry nods, but let's stay awhile.
In hues of chaos, fruits are ablaze,
With grapes in a tussle, they start their play.

Apples debate who's the juiciest prize,
While pears roll their eyes and offer a sigh.
A banana slips, what a hilarious fall,
Yet they all laugh and bounce back, one and all.

The tablecloth giggles beneath the feast,
As flowers sway, sharing stories at least.
Each shape and color, a character bold,
In this vibrant scene, the laughter unfolds.

So let this tableau bring smiles to your face,
Where stillness transforms into comedic grace.
In every brushstroke, a chuckle is spun,
Art and humor unite, oh what fun!

Echoes from the Hearth

In a cozy nook where laughter thrives,
Pots and pans sing like silly hives.
With spoons as conductors, stirring the cheer,
A symphony of clanking, oh what a year!

Baking cookies with a sprinkle of joy,
Flour fights break out, causing a ploy.
Whisking and mixing with giggles and glee,
As chocolate chips waltz, just wait and see.

Dishes join in with a rattling sound,
As laughter spins 'round, so freely abound.
In the warmth of the hearth, each moment's a prize,
With echoes of chuckles, like firefly skies.

So gather around, share stories with love,
With pots and pans singing just like a dove.
In this lively kitchen, joy never departs,
As the echoes of laughter warm all our hearts.

Crafted Echoes of Floral Muse

In a corner, a pot starts to sing,
A tune about daisies, with flair and a swing.
It tiptoes on jokes, like a clumsy ballet,
While tulips all giggle, putting on quite the play.

With petals a-twirl, they dance in the breeze,
A chorus of colors, oh, how they tease!
The sun joins the fun with a glimmering wink,
While bees form a band, on the brink of a drink.

Old ceramic faces crack smiles, oh so wide,
As laughter spills out, like a bubbly tide.
Each bloom has a secret, a humorous tale,
Of how they defied the notorious snail.

In this whimsical world where blossoms convene,
Every silly notion is vibrant and keen.
So next time you pass that pot on your shelf,
Remember the laughter that blooms by itself.

Sunlit Silhouettes of Memory

Sunshine spills laughter on walls made of clay,
Where shadows play pranks, in a silly ballet.
A cactus attempts to initiate cheer,
While roses roll their eyes, 'Oh, not this year!'

The daisies concoct a lighthearted jest,
'Look at us thriving, we're simply the best!'
While violets whisper, 'Oh, what a bold claim,'
As daisies blurt out, 'What's in a name?'

Pots in a row, with smiles that could gleam,
They're all in on giggles, a colorful dream.
With roots firmly planted, they share their delight,
As buds share their gossip from morning till night.

In this sunny space where shadows collide,
Every quirk and flicker brings joy multiplied.
So hang up your worries, let laughter accrue,
In this garden of memory, there's fun (not woo-woo!).

Liquid Luminescence in Terra

A teapot whispers to a jug with a grin,
'Your spout's looking crooked, now that's quite a win!'
With chuckles bubbling up from inside their form,
They toast to each mishap and every soft norm.

Poured tea tickles petals, a sparkly dance,
Each sip is a giggle, a jovial trance.
Mugs splash in smiles, with coffee so bright,
While teacups vote 'tea is the drink of the night.'

The kettle joins in, with a sizzle and pop,
Says, 'Join in the fun, let's never stop!'
As sugar cubes tumble, a sweet bagatelle,
Spinning around in a miniature well.

In this liquid chorus where joy seems to bloom,
Every clink is a chuckle, dispelling all gloom.
So pour out your worries in cups stacked high,
And laugh with the flavors that never run dry.

Fragments of Fragile Stories

Once upon a pot, a story did weave,
Of petals and laughter, it's hard to believe.
With handles that wiggle and bases that sway,
Each piece holds a memory, gleefully gay.

A teacup claimed bravely, 'I'm fancy and grand!'
While a chipped little mug tried to give it a hand.
They giggled and bantered, trading sweet quips,
As saucers spun tales of long-lost trips.

Pans in a corner joined with a chime,
In sync with the echoes of playful rhyme.
Each fragment had humor and stories to share,
Plus dreams from the past, floating light as air.

So here in this circle of laughter and clay,
Where stories are shared in a silly ballet,
Embrace all the quirks through this playful spree,
For life's but a canvas, bright-fragmented glee.

The Harmony of Form

In a shop where oddities dwell,
Containers jive, oh what a spell!
One's a pitcher, the other's a jar,
Together they dance, like a quirky bazaar.

Frogs in bow ties, cats with glee,
They host a ball, come and see!
Spilling out laughter, they swish and sway,
Charmed by the quirks of their sprightly ballet.

Wobbly edges, paint gone awry,
But they don't fret as they slyly cry.
"Who needs perfection in form or line?"
Let's laugh at the flaws, they're truly divine!

So gather around, grab a cup of cheer,
In this riot of colors, there's nothing to fear.
For each misfit and mishap, we toast with a grin,
In this vase-filled realm, let the fun times begin!

Imbued Fluency

Words can wiggle, they slip and slide,
Just like a vase that's too much pride.
It tries to hold all, but tips in a rush,
Spilling its secrets in a colorful hush.

Rhymes hop around like beans in a pod,
Contorting themselves, oh how they nod!
"Catch me if you can," they merrily sing,
In a vessel's embrace, they frolic and bling.

With quotes from the quirky and hints of the wise,
Each line comes alive, oh what a surprise!
From porcelain whispers to tin can dreams,
They swirl through the air, like giggles in streams.

So raise your glasses, toast to the spree,
To words that bewilder, and jars full of glee.
For in this potpourri of ain't-that-funny,
Life's a wacky garden, and it's ever so sunny!

Wandering with Petals

Petals drift like thoughts on a breeze,
Landing soft on containers with ease.
Each sweet aroma brings a chuckle too,
While the flower's vase winks and giggles anew.

One day a daisy, quite sprightly and bold,
Thought it could dance, being happily rolled.
It tumbled and twirled, causing quite a clatter,
Said the tulip nearby, "Oh, here comes the splatter!"

"Stick to your roots, dear," the geranium said,
But the daisy just laughed, "Come join me instead!"
So they spun and they spun, with petals a-flutter,
Making all the neighbors giggle and stutter.

Leaves joined the party, all green and spry,
While succulents nodded, with a glimmering eye.
Who knew that these pots brimmed so with fun?
With petals and laughter, they danced 'til the sun!

Graced by Growth

In charming corners where laughter bloomed,
Containers overflow, happily consumed.
Each pot has a story, each has a flare,
They giggle and wiggle in the sunlit air.

Oh, how they grow, like jokes fresh and spry,
Roots reaching deep, toward the sky!
"Water me more!" a juvenile vase cries,
As friends butt in, "Keep it low, don't be wise!"

So tipsy they are with a hint of wild,
Dripping with whimsy, just like a child.
They thrive on the clutter, the smiles, and the fun,
In this lively assembly, they'll never be done.

So here's to their growth, in joy intertwined,
Containers and blossoms, in laughter combined.
For in every slip and every soft beam,
They flourish together, a whimsical dream!

www.ingramcontent.com/pod-product-compliance
Lightning Source LLC
Chambersburg PA
CBHW070318120526
44590CB00017B/2729